Contents

The Ramblers' Association promotes country walking, protects rights of way, campaigns for access to open country, woodlands, etc. and defends the beauty of the landscape. The RA plays a major role in securing legislation to protect our paths and countryside. Please give your support by becoming a member. Write to: The Ramblers' Association, 1/5 Wandsworth Road, London SW8 2XX. Tel: 0171 339 8500. FAX: 0171 339 8501.

Berkshire Area
The RA has seven Groups across the County. Each Group arranges its own extensive programme of walks and endeavours to monitor local footpaths, to seek improvements and oppose any threats to them. For details contact: Mr John Moules, 50 Qualitas, Roman Hill, Bracknell, Berkshire RG12 7QG.

Maps in this book are based upon Ordnance Survey maps with permission of the Controller of the Stationery Office. Crown copyright reserved. 43408U.

Coopers Hill and Runnymede

This circular walk visits the wooded slopes of Coopers Hill with its memorials to Second World War airmen, President Kennedy and the Magna Carta; follows the Thames Path downstream for 1½ miles and passes along the edge of Runnymede.

Distance: 4 miles

Start: Memorial (free) car park in Coopers Hill Lane, Englefield Green. Grid ref: 996 718

From entrance to car park turn left along Coopers Hill Lane. Follow red-brick wall past the main entrance to Brunel University's Runnymede Campus and past houses beyond. At main road junction ahead, at top of Priest Hill, turn right downhill, on roadside verge for some 200 yards, then turn right into tree-lined drive (Oak Lane). Where drive divides go straight on between brick pillars, soon entering woodland on gravel path descending to JFK Memorial.

Cloister of the Air Forces Memorial

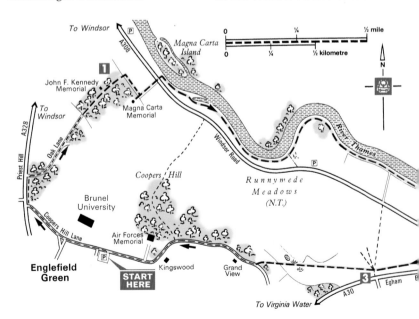

Magna Carta Memorial

1 Continue downhill on unusual granite-set pathway and, emerging from trees by wooden swing-gate, turn right along edge of Runnymede (NT) for nearly 200 yards to the Magna Carta Memorial – erected by the American Bar Association. Now turn left across meadow with wire fence on right and with great care cross main road (A308). Facing the River Thames, opposite Magna Carta Island, turn right along well-defined riverside path, gravel at first. After some 200 yards *keep right* of tree-fringed backwater and continue beside river for a further 1½ miles downstream to Bell Weir Lock.

2 Beyond lock continue on riverbank to just before road bridges ahead (the far one carries the M25) and turn right on gravel path to reach road (A30) after metal gate. Here turn right along footway passing front of Runnymede Hotel and Spa to reach the memorials and small buildings marking the entrance to Runnymede (NT). Here with care turn left to

cross road (A308) and head half-right across the grass on a line which soon follows left side of meadow with Egham bypass (A30) nearby on left.

3 Cross over end of tarmac path and bear slightly right, away from bypass, towards *highest point* of Coopers Hill (not along paths 8, 13, or 15!). This well-defined grass path runs straight to footbridge and swing-gate at foot of hill. Maintain same direction steeply up hill to cross further stile and turn right up a sunken, rough and stony track. Pass property on left, Grand View, to emerge eventually from woodland at the top of Coopers Hill. Follow road round bends, beside trimmed holly hedge and turn off right to visit the Air Forces Memorial – a beautiful and peaceful cloister recording the names of 20,000 airmen who died during the Second World War and who have no known graves.

The Memorial provides excellent views over the flat countryside to the north. Continue along the road a further 250 yards to return to start.

DATE WALKED		

Colne Brook and Ankerwycke Estate

This circular walk is within sight of water for much of its length. Meandering through the village of Wraysbury, it follows the Colne Brook for about a mile, returning along the Thames-side meadows of Ankerwycke Farm. The circular route is made possible by the 'Permitted Path' across Windsor & Maidenhead Council's Ankerwycke Estate.

Distance: 4½ miles
Start: Free car park north side of The Green at Wraysbury. Grid ref: 003 742 Alternatively start at Wraysbury Station.

Leaving main entrance of car park turn right along road (The Green) and shortly after footbridge adjacent to ford, at The Perseverance, turn right along road (High Street) for about 65 yards to Baptist Church. Here turn left across road to enter through metal swing-gate a fenced path, soon with gravel lake on right and gardens on left.

Follow this grass path through remains of metal gate and along a hedged strip leading to buildings of Tithe Farm and continue on gravel track to road ahead. Now turn right along road and on approaching railway bridge, for safety, fork right along road to station and cross railway by both flights of pedestrian steps.

1 After leaving station car park, cross road bridge over Colne Brook and immediately turn right over small footbridge, to follow riverside path with fence of Wraysbury Reservoir on left and Colne Brook and then railway on right. On eventually reaching level crossing, with care turn right over stile and railway line. With back to line, bear left for some 75 yards, then bear right towards taller trees. Path (No.4) winds ahead, soon

between Colne Brook nearby on right and lake to left.

Follow this path for well over ½ mile to reach stile and steps at road. Before climbing this stile, turn left for a few yards to see the pedestal erected in August 1832, recording an interesting court action over the rights to pen up the waters of the River Colne. Now turn right along the road to cross the Colne again and continue on right-hand footway of Staines Road. (At road junction notice Ferry Lane opposite, a public right of way to the old Bell Weir Ferry).

2 Now follow Staines Road for nearly ½ mile, past houses at first, then tree-lined, using grass verge and then tarmac path. Reaching two houses on left of road, carefully cross over, passing to right of No. 104, to enter fenced 'Permitted Path' leading to north bank of River Thames opposite Runnymede.

3 Turning right, follow riverbank, partly on gravel path, and on eventually emerging from trees,

Parish Church of St Andrew, Wraysbury

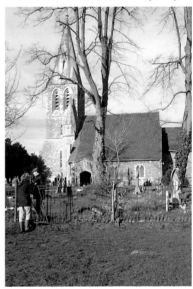

continue ahead along edge of fields with fence and river on left. Among the trees on far right-hand side of the second field was once the site of a priory (founded 1160) for Benedictine nuns – here please do not stray from the path. Also look across the river to the wooded slopes of Coopers Hill with its Air Forces Memorial. Below the hill are the meadows where King John signed the Magna Carta on 15 June 1215. These sites are visited on Ramble 1.

Cross stile and footbridge at end of field and after 50 yards in trees and a second stile, join fenced path soon turning away from river, eventually to reach road (Magna Carta Lane). Now turn right along road for 60 yards, then left over stile to follow edge of field with fence on left. After

gap in fence and footbridge at end of field, maintain same direction in next field towards distant church.

4 After two stiles close together at field boundary enter wire-fenced path and beyond further stile continue with fence on left and ditch on right. After next stile pass through middle of small field to enter by metal swing-gate the churchyard of Wraysbury Parish Church of St Andrew. Pass to right of church and from lych-gate go ahead along road to T-junction (Windsor Road). Cross over and turn right, and just after The George bear left into The Green (note village sign on corner) to return to start.

DATE WALKED		

Romney Lock and Eton College

This circular walk includes all of the Thames Path at Windsor and passes through the historic buildings of Eton College. Within the route is a shorter alternative of barely 2 miles which includes the length of Eton High Street, little changed in appearance since the 18th century, with buildings dating back to 1420.

Distance: 2 or 5 miles
Start: Windsor Bridge.
Grid ref: 967 772

With your back to Windsor Castle cross the pedestrianised early Victorian cast-iron bridge spanning the River Thames and turn left into Brocas Street. After 50 yards go *straight ahead* as road narrows, passing to right of Eton College boat-house. From here join the riverside path across The Brocas – meadows given to Eton College some 500 years ago by a former Provost, Henry Bost.

1 Continue along the riverside path beneath Brunel's railway bridge (1849) and shortly, just in front of green footbridge ahead, bear right, away from river now with trees and back-water on left. In corner of field go left along lane for about 100 yards. Here, by Swan Lifeline, turn right, across open fields to junction with path from left where they both pass under viaduct. Now go left on tarmac track for some 50 yards, then maintain same direction over playing field, shortly to cross road (B3026). Now go straight on, keeping close to right-hand boundary, pass through a wooden swing-gate and continue bearing right to end of open area. Join tarmac drive ahead to road and continue (Common Lane) to emerge facing Eton College. The College was founded by King Henry VI in 1440. The buildings and cloisters are open to visitors in summer until 4.30 pm.

2 For the *shorter walk* turn right along the length of Eton High Street back to Windsor Bridge. For the *longer route* go straight across the road and through the archway ahead, following the footway skirting to left of the main college buildings and through a second arch. At end of buildings on right, bear half-left on wide stony path across the playing fields. At brick bridge fork right, on narrower path. With road ahead turn right (without crossing it) on path, fenced at first. Where road swings left go straight ahead through metal gate. In front of boat-house look for stile close to corner of building and take this path over waste land. Cross minor road with stiles both sides and go on through paddock, then over concrete bridge and after wooden gate duck under railway viaduct.

Now bear right, leading onto Datchet Golf Course and follow right-hand boundary. After property on right

Windsor Castle from The Brocas

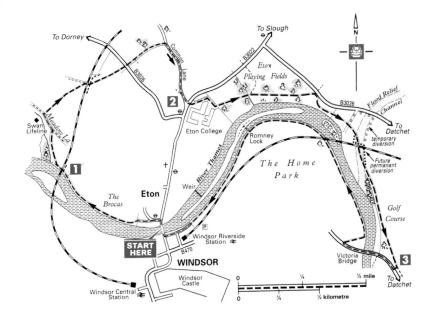

continue until some 50 yards beyond a triple-bunker turn right to leave course, up concrete steps in hedge to road.

3 Turn right along footway over Victoria Bridge (built in 1851 – note plaques on parapet). On other side of bridge turn right across the greensward of the Home Park – the scene each May of the famous Royal Windsor Horse Show. With river on right follow the bank for a little over a mile back to Windsor Bridge with a possible detour to Romney Lock. On the way pass under Black Potts railway bridge where Thames Path continues across a field, through a boat-yard, then to right of green building. (Turn right over bridge in boat-yard to visit the lock and the original tow-path, called Cobblers Path, now on the lock island.)

Thames Path becomes a roadway until by footbridge over railway we bear right into Romney Walk, leading to The Donkey House and back to the start.

DATE WALKED		

The Cockpit, Eton

Great Common and Conker Alley

This circular walk crosses Eton Great Common and follows the Thames Path for about a mile, returning along the edge of Dorney Common, with a shorter alternative beside South Field.

Distance: 2½ or 4 miles
Start: Service road opposite Shepherds Hut in Eton Wick. Grid ref: 947 785

Facing Shepherds Hut turn left along Eton Wick Road for a few yards, then left again, into Bell Lane. Shortly, at bend in road, turn sharp right along green strip beside ditch on left (or use the gravel path). Join road and continue ahead until this divides. Take left fork (cul-de-sac) and just before left-hand bend, turn right over stile beside gate, onto Eton Great Common.

1 Keep along left side of Common, near tree-lined Common Ditch and pass under road bridge (A332). Continue ahead, go under railway viaduct in front and immediately turn right onto 'shared-use' path. Cross road ahead where tarmac path skirts left of allotments before rejoining viaduct. At this point turn right through arch, then immediately bear half-left on mid-field bridleway to emerge by Swan Lifeline Centre (Cuckoo Weir Island).

2 Here turn right along hedged track which leads under road bridge to reach open fields ahead with multiplicity of signs! Take the second path from left, cross-field, towards distant seat beside trees where field-path merges with the Thames Path, with Windsor racecourse on opposite bank. Much of the towpath here was resurfaced and widened some years ago as a 'shared use' path, originally for walkers and cyclists but now equally convenient for wheelchair users.

Stay on the riverside until just before concrete footbridge, our *shorter circuit* turns away from river and heads directly back to the start at Eton Wick. The *longer route* continues along the riverside towards Boveney Lock. Just a few yards before the lock turn away from the river across a tarmac area and into a chestnut tree-lined drive (Conker Alley), soon catching a glimpse of Boveney's tiny 13th-century chapel of St Mary Magdalene across field to left.

Cygnets on Boveney Ditch

Footbridge onto Dorney Common

3 At end of field on right turn right along field-edge path and follow this to far corner. Here turn right, now with stream (Cress Brook) on left, soon to reach and cross footbridge onto Common. Now bear right to road at cattle grid. Pass through swing-gate and cross road to follow grass verge and path for about ¼ mile to return to start.

DATE WALKED		

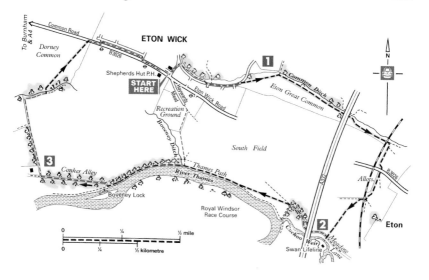

Boveney Chapel and Dorney Common

This circular walk follows the Thames Path for nearly 2 miles, passing Oakley Court and Bray Studios, visiting Dorney village and returning across Dorney Common. With completion of the flood relief channel under construction (planned for 2001), a new car park and adjacent paths will become available – see map.

Distance: 5 miles

Start: Free car park at Boveney (provided by Eton College). Grid ref: 939 777

Leave car park through swing-gate in back corner. Turn right along short enclosed path past Boveney's tiny 13th-century Chapel of St Mary Magdalene and turn right along the Thames Path.

Soon pass Eton College's modern boat-house and after a sharp right-hand bend in the river, notice on far side Windsor Marina.

Next to appear on the opposite bank, behind immaculate lawns to the water's edge, is Oakley Court Hotel. This fine Victorian Gothic mansion of 1858, set in 35 acres of beautifully maintained gardens, was rescued from certain destruction when planners allowed work to commence in 1980 to restore the derelict listed building as a luxury hotel.

Then, after some riverside bungalows on far bank, is another interesting historic group of buildings, the 18th-century Down Place, with distinctive clock tower and cupola. Once the meeting place of the infamous Kit-Kat Club, it is now the home of Bray Studios.

1 Immediately opposite Bray Marina turn right, away from river along path beside hedgerow. At this point, a few yards further along the river, notice the new 'conveyor bridge' opened in 1997 to transport part of the 4½ million tonnes of gravel to create Eton College's 2 km-long rowing lake. Due for completion in 2007, costing over £10 million, the facility will include a nature reserve and arboretum.

Follow the way-marked gravel path, over a footbridge, until finally emerging at bend in road. Cross road ahead and use the footway (Court Lane). Shortly turn right into short cul-de-sac if you wish to visit the part 12th-century

Cress Brook, Dorney Common

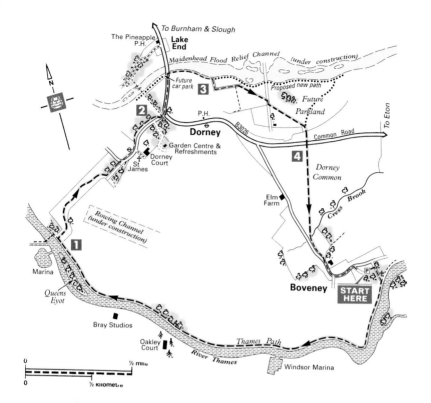

brick and flint-faced St James's Church and for a glimpse of the charming half-timbered Tudor Dorney Court. Built around 1440, it has been the home of the Palmer family since 1628. To ease the burden of maintaining this wonderful old house, the Palmers decided in 1981 to open their historic home during the summer to visitors. For times, telephone (01628) 604638. 'Dorney' means Island of Bees and although Dorney Court still claims fame for its honey, it is probably better known for producing the first pineapple in England which was presented to Charles II in 1661.

2 Continue to end of Court Lane. When the flood relief channel is finished, the field-edge path on left here will access an alternative route – see map. In the meantime, turn left along footway of Lake End Road. Just after left-hand bend, cross to stile to join path beside new channel.

3 Soon the original path turns right, then left, following field boundary. Disregard first path turning right but after a further 50 yards turn half-right across open field. Near far corner cross stile, then concrete track, to continue in same direction, now along enclosed path. This passes close to buildings of Manor Farm and bears right to stile at edge of Dorney Common.

4 Cross road in front and head straight over common, aiming right of distant trees. On far side join road to cross bridge over stream (Cress Brook). Continue along roadside edge of common, bearing left after Boveney Court Farm to return to car park at start.

DATE WALKED		

Brunel Bridge and Bray Village

This circular walk passes Bray Lock and Monkey Island, crosses the new 'conveyor bridge' over the River Thames before returning through Bray village and along the Green Way.

Distance: 5 miles

Start: Small (free) car park in Guards Club Park (closed at dusk), accessed via Oldfield Road and Oldacres. Grid ref: 901 811

Explore this secluded little riverside park (fine view of Maidenhead Bridge from the island), and then leave through side gate past one-time Guards Club, now Reitlingen Lodge. Follow narrow road ahead (Guards Club Road) to Riviera Hotel, turn right over Maidenhead Bridge and then right again, into River Road.

Immediately on left look out for dragons lurking on the rooftops! These were made locally at the old Maidenhead Brick & Tile Works at Pinkneys Green. Join Thames Path by Maidenhead's splendid new rowing club and shortly pass under the Sounding Arch of Brunel's rail bridge, noting plaque on south side. This is one of the best-known bridges in the country, depicted by Turner in his famous painting 'Rain, Steam and Speed'.

1 Continue along riverside until, before the last property, Harefield, turn left along gravel drive, becoming a narrow path beside an evergreen hedge. Pass wooden swing-gate and follow grass path through three fields ahead. Then after gateway, bear left to continue in same direction as before but now diagonally across middle of larger field, aiming for right-hand end of hedgerow trees on far side. Here join tarmac drive and at junction just ahead, bear right. Reaching a junction, facing Amerden Lodge, turn right to riverside (just downstream from Bray Lock).

2 Now turn left, on Thames Path again, shortly to pass under concrete road bridge (M4). Soon look right for Monkey Island, with its fishing lodge and pavilion built for the third Duke of Marlborough in 1774. It probably derives its name from the monkey paintings on the ceiling of one of the rooms in the present hotel. The next feature is the bridge opened in 1997 to carry part of the 4½ million tonnes of sand and gravel being excavated to form Eton College's 2 kilometre-long rowing lake.

The Sounding Arch

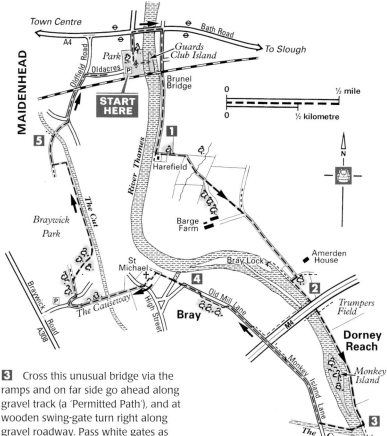

3 Cross this unusual bridge via the ramps and on far side go ahead along gravel track (a 'Permitted Path'), and at wooden swing-gate turn right along gravel roadway. Pass white gates as drive becomes tree-lined and at road ahead keep straight along footway of motorway bridge, descending into Monkey Island Lane, where possible using path beneath roadside trees.

4 Where road bends left go straight on into tarmac path in front of black and white terrace called Bettoney Vere. At road ahead, facing Tansy Cottage, turn left then immediately right, leading into churchyard of the famous 13th-century parish church of St Michael, Bray. (Remember 'The Vicar of Bray' and all that!) Pass left of church, out through gateway and turn right along High Street for some 30 yards, then bear left beside green, becoming tree-lined tarmac path known as The Causeway. Where Causeway meets road junction turn

right for some 50 yards, then cross into path beside wooden gate. At path junction shortly ahead, turn right over footbridge and within 20 yards bear left, signed Braywick Park/Green Way, along tree-lined path. Pass beside a locked gate and carry on as track widens to roadway.

5 Cross bridge over canal (The Cut) and straight on to roadside. Here carefully cross over and bear left along footway of Oldfield Road. Go under railway bridge, take first turning right, Oldacres, and follow this ahead to return to car park at start.

DATE WALKED		

Widbrook Common and Cliveden Reach

This circular walk goes out through the area near **Sheephouse Farm**, crosses **Widbrook Common (NT)** and continues northwards to reach Cookham village. The return route includes Cliveden Reach, 1½ miles of the Thames Path, opposite the beautiful Hanging Woods of the National Trust's Cliveden Estate.

Distance: 5½ miles
Start: Free car park in Lower Cookham Road (A4094) near Boulters Lock. Grid ref: 902 825

With your back to river, leave car park at far left-hand corner and turn left along Boulters Lane. At road junction ahead, with care turn right along Ray Mill Road East, then immediately after second turning on right, The Pagoda, turn half-right along fenced path and cross over Sheephouse Road ahead into Summerleaze Road. When this road turns sharp left, turn right for a few paces, then immediately left over metal stile. As a result of a decision (1998) to create vehicular access to North Maidenhead Cricket Club, some changes will occur here. But until then follow path beside wire fence of gravel plant on right.

1 After left-hand turn, cross footbridge and continue along grassy bank beside stream. At path junction turn sharp right over footbridge, joining the Green Way – a 5-mile waterside corridor from Bray to Cookham. From here take the East (right) fork across middle of this rough field. On far side go through gap in hedge and head along mid-field path to remains of metal stile. Leave field and bear right along gravel farm-track until, just before metal field gates ahead, turn left on mid-field path to stile in hedge and a 1934 Maidenhead Borough boundary stone, at the edge of Widbrook Common.

This enclosed 65-acre Common is preserved by the National Trust. Under the supervision of the Hayward, commoners graze their cattle from mid-May to mid-November for a seasonal fee, the rent going to Cookham Educational Charity, set up in the past for apprentice boys.

2 To continue the walk cross footbridge ahead (White Brook), where path divides. Go straight ahead to cross stile in left-hand field corner, then follow field-edge with railings on right at first. After railings finish, turn right along edge of two fields, with trees and Strand Water on left. Cross farm-track ahead, bear right over stile and follow side of field with railings on left – here observe Cliveden House (NT) among distant trees at top of woodland ridge on right. Path narrows at small copse and turns half-left eventually to emerge at Cookham Moor.

3 Facing War Memorial turn right along School Lane and at the end carefully cross Sutton Road (A4094) into Mill Lane opposite. At end of lane, walk just past Mill House, turn right, then immediately left, to join winding path through woodland strip down to the river and site of the long-ceased My Lady Ferry. Now turn right along one of the most beautiful stretches of the Thames – Cliveden Reach.

Opposite the first small island, high up on the edge of the Hanging Woods of the Cliveden Estate, a memorial viewpoint was established in 1992 in memory of Peter Nevell who originated these walks. The panorama across the river towards Cookham, with the distant prospect of Ashley Hill and Hurley, was an area of countryside in which he took particular interest. Peter was also a member and voluntary warden with the National Trust.

4 About halfway along the towpath, at the start of an avenue of riverside trees, notice another boundary stone on right, at end of wooden fence. Eventually, after about 1½ miles along the towpath, you return to Lower Cookham Road and car park at start.

DATE WALKED		

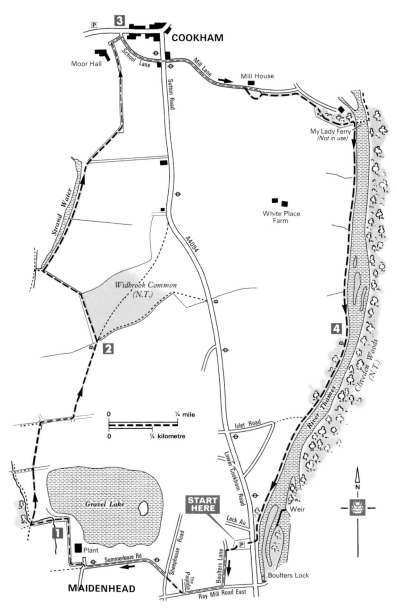

**Help Protect
Public Paths and
Common Land**

THE
**OPEN SPACES
SOCIETY**

Write to: 25a Bell Street, Henley-on-Thames, Oxon RG9 2BA

Marsh Meadow and Cockmarsh

This circular walk follows the Berkshire bank of the River Thames for well over a mile and does a complete circuit of Cockmarsh (National Trust) – 132 acres of flat marshy meadows and steep chalk slopes – designated an SSSI.

Distance: 3½ miles
Start: National Trust (free) car park on The Moor at Cookham. Grid ref: 893 854

With your back to road, turn right across The Moor to turn left at concrete stile beside first cottage ahead. Follow edge of field (Marsh Meadow) to wooden swing-gate in corner. Cross drives to both Sailing Club and Winterbourne and turn left into broad gravel track leading to river. Now turn left and follow river bank for about ¾ mile to railway bridge. Here pass through swing-gate and keep to water's edge with riverside bungalows on left. At end of bungalows pass through wooden gate and follow riverside meadow forming the northern edge of Cockmarsh.

Cockmarsh is part of the Maidenhead and Cookham Commons (total 848 acres) which, with the Lordship of the Manor, were acquired for £2,800 by public subscription in 1934 and handed over to the National Trust to be managed by a local preservation committee. On Cockmarsh are five ancient burial mounds, only one being discernible.

1 In the next field, reaching the white building at water's edge, Ferry Cottage – the spot where a ferry once crossed to the Bucks bank at Spade Oak – bear left away from river. On reaching corner of roadway ahead, turn left on cross-field track to stile

A field of yellow oilseed rape next to Cockmarsh

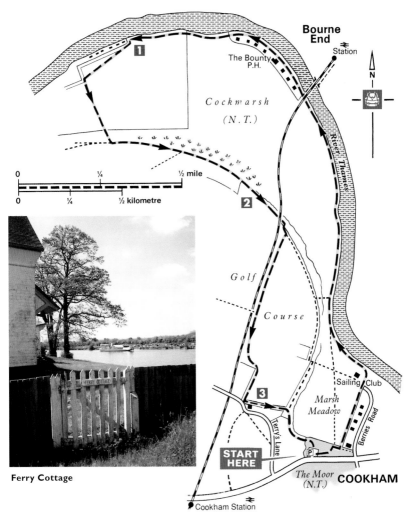

Ferry Cottage

by gate. Go ahead to foot of hill and turn left on green track with steep slope on right and marshland on left.

2 Reaching stile, continue ahead on track beside tree-lined slope on left. Pass under railway arch, cross stile in fence on right, then continue ahead for some yards before turning right up steps to follow edge of John Lewis Golf Course, with trees and railway on right. Stay on the path along this side of the course, finally to reach stile at end − along here look left for the river, Cookham village and bridge, and Cliveden Estate (NT) among woodland beyond.

3 At end of gravel track, some six yards before junction with Terry's Lane, turn left down very narrow hedged path (not the wide one), beside white bungalow. Enter meadow ahead over stile and bear right down slope to follow willow-fringed ditch on left, then at end of field cross stile and footbridge to arrive back at The Moor and car park at start.

DATE WALKED		

Hillgrove Farm and Spade Oak Reach

This circular walk, after crossing the John Lewis Golf Course, passes through the high farmland around Cookham Dean before descending for a full circuit of Cockmarsh (National Trust) and returning along well over a mile of the Thames Path.

Distance: 4½ miles
Start: Cookham War Memorial.
Grid ref: 893 854

With your back to War Memorial, cross end of School Lane and walk the length of the old raised road across The Moor. This causeway has existed here since 1770 and the brick bridge over the Fleet Ditch (midway) was a gift to the village in 1929, replacing many which had been swept away in times of flood. Where roads merge turn right into Terry's Lane. At last house on left, Tremayne, fork left into rising fenced path. Rejoining Terry's Lane, continue for some 30 yards, then bear right up gravel track to enter at stile the John Lewis Golf Course (completed in 1976 for the benefit of the employees of the Partnership).

1 Follow well-used path along edge of course, soon with railway line nearby, shortly to turn left over railway bridge. Continue straight ahead through middle of golf course, slowly climbing with care, passing to right of distant grey building and eventually to follow fence and trees on left.

2 At top corner of field turn left along fenced path beside drive, leading to road (Terry's Lane). Here with care cross road and stile opposite. Keep fence on right and at further stile bear right, still beside fence, leading to stile next to gate, opposite the white buildings of Hillgrove Farm. Here cross over (at junction of Alleyns Lane and Bradcutts Lane) to enter, by stile opposite, broad fenced path between paddocks. Path narrows between fences and after a stile maintains same direction ahead along wide grass strip, to reach road after two stiles close together. With care turn left along road for some 70 yards and then, immediately before start of metal railings on right, fork right down narrow woodland path. At the bottom turn right down gravel track, soon to enter by stile next to gate, Cockmarsh, N.T. – 132 acres of flat marshy meadows and steep chalk slopes designated an SSSI.

3 Just beyond stile keep right along track for a further 130 yards where there is a choice of route. The walk continues downhill (with fine views over Spade Oak Reach), but the young and agile may take the grass path to the right along the top of the ridge (with even better views) before taking the very steep broad grass path between bushes to rejoin route at bottom of hill.

4 At bottom of hill cross stile beside gate and head between fields towards the river. On far side turn right along wide grass strip with field on right, towards white building, Ferry Cottage – the spot where a ferry once crossed to the Bucks bank at Spade Oak.

5 Now follow water's edge for nearly 1½ miles, then where river bears left, roughly half-way between a large solitary tree on the riverbank and Cookham Sailing Club enclosure ahead, bear right through middle of open field (Marsh Meadow). On far side leave field at wooden swing-gate, turn left along edge of The Moor past the Crown to return to start.

DATE WALKED		

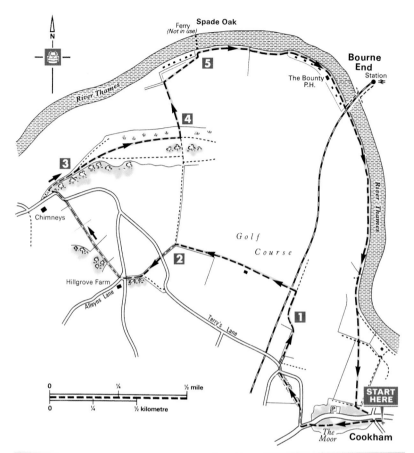

N

River Thames

Spade Oak

Ferry
(Not in use)

5

Bourne
End

Station

The Bounty
P.H.

River Thames

4

3

Chimneys

Hillgrove Farm

Alleyns Lane

2

Golf Course

Terry's Lane

1

0   ¼   ½ mile

0   ¼   ½ kilometre

START
HERE

P

*The
Moor*

Cookham

David Maclean, Minister of State for the Environment and Countryside officially opens a new kissing gate at Cockmarsh, provided by the East Berkshire RA group. May 1993.

Ronald Wood and Fern

This circular walk tolerates some urban fringe paths around Flackwell Heath, but is adequately compensated by the slopes, woodland and fields overlooking the Thames Valley, plus a short but interesting section of the river itself. The route is easily accessible by rail.

Distance: 4½ miles
Start: Bourne End railway station. Grid ref: 894 872

With your back to the station, carefully cross main road and head along Boston Drive. After some 80 yards, at building on right, Eghams Court, turn right into path skirting car park and then between fences. At end of path turn left and carefully cross Cores End Road. Then turn left for a few yards before passing through gap in fence on right.

Follow well-used path (old railway line) between banks. At end of houses on right, at path junction, turn left up slope into right-hand way-marked path winding through rough grass to stile at field boundary. Maintain same direction in field ahead, soon beside hedge on left. In top corner of field at stile beside metal gate, path continues with hedge now on right, with fine views (on clear days!) especially back left towards the Thames and slopes beyond N.T. Cockmarsh.

1 At top corner of this large field, turn left beside Ronald Wood. Cross stile beneath overhead cables and keep right, along broad tree-lined path. Shortly fork right to enter narrow fenced path between houses. Cross end of cul-de-sac and continue ahead on path between houses and woodland to reach the Green Dragon.

Cross Blind Lane, pass to right of pub and along length of Green Dragon Lane to Chapman Lane. Here cross into path opposite and follow wall on left through right and left bends, then down steep slope before bearing left to stile in bottom corner of trees. Keeping fence on left, follow side of three fields to Pigeonhouse Farm. Facing farmhouse turn right down short tarmac drive to road (Sheepridge Lane).

2 Here cross road and go ahead along farm track. At top of rise ahead, bear left diagonally across field and on far side bear left down lane. Where this turns right, go ahead on gravel track leading into Fern Lane Cemetery. Keep to left-hand path, and just before leaving by swing-gate, notice tallest white cross to right, the grave of Edgar Wallace. Grass path beside railings leads to road. Carefully turn right, using grass verge where possible, to road junction. Again with care, cross road (A4155), turn left for some 75 yards, then right, into Coldmoorholm Lane towards Spade Oak.

After right-hand turn in road, at start of next left-hand bend, enter path on right for some 10 yards, then turn left over wooden footbridge and along wire-fenced path, beside field on right, to emerge at road, opposite the Spade Oak Hotel.

3 Now turn right along road and immediately after crossing stream bear left along Upper Thames Way to reach and cross railway line. Shortly, at riverside, turn left and follow public path through Sailing Club and then Marina. Just beyond Marina office building, where roadway turns away from riverside, follow Thames Path through iron swing-gate beside a Victorian house.

Follow path across gardens of houses on left until, some 15 yards beyond the railway bridge (which today also carries the Thames Path), turn left through gate in railings and up steps to follow rail line to return to start. (If gate is locked continue on public footpath to main road.)

DATE WALKED		

Path through the Sailing Club

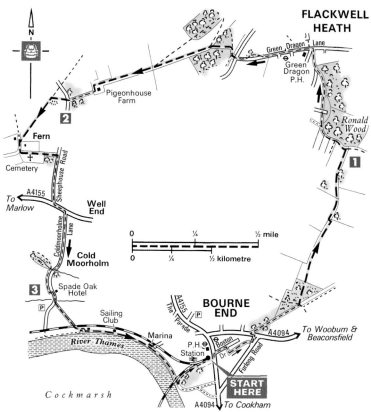

FLACKWELL HEATH

Green Dragon Lane

Green Dragon P.H.

Ronald Wood

Pigeonhouse Farm

1

2

Fern

Cemetery

Sheephouse Road

To Marlow

A4155

Well End

Coldmoorholme Lane

↓ **Cold Moorholm**

0   ¼   ½ mile

0   ¼   ½ kilometre

3

Spade Oak Hotel

P

Sailing Club

Marina

River Thames

The Parade

A4155

P

BOURNE END

A4094

To Wooburn & Beaconsfield

P.H.

Station

Boston Dr

Furlong Road

START HERE

Cockmarsh

A4094 ↓ *To Cookham*

N

Little Marlow and Riverwoods

This circular walk, after leaving the eastern outskirts of Marlow and passing through a modern business area (Globe Park), follows a pleasant farm road into the attractive village of Little Marlow. From here, a tree-lined path leads to the River Thames, and the walk returns along a 1½ mile stretch of the river, opposite the slopes of Winter Hill and Quarry Wood and through the Riverwoods public open space.

Distance: 4 miles
Start: Riverside (free) car park in Gossmore Lane, Marlow. Grid ref: 859 862

With your back to the river, walk along car park access drive, then turn right along Gossmore Lane. Where road bends to go under Marlow-Bisham bypass, turn left to cross railway line through swing-gates.
1 Continue ahead along Fieldhouse Lane, then turn first right into Parkway. Follow this road through the modern business area (Globe Park), keeping to pavement on left.
2 Soon after the big Tektronix building, reach and cross footbridge ahead, over dual carriageway (A404). From footbridge go straight ahead, shortly bearing left along track with glimpses of gravel lake on right. Keep straight on, over two drives to mansion and buildings (of Westhorpe House), then continue straight on along fenced track between fields. Cross a lane and on into a gated estate road which leads, after about ½ mile, to the Queen's Head and Little Marlow.
3 Now turn right along village street (Church Road), passing in turn the Manor House and the picturesque 800 year-old flint-faced Parish Church of St John the Baptist. (Notice the

Towpath opposite Quarry Wood

unusual 'double' lych-gate.) Pass left of timber-framed Manor Farm into private road (a public path), then after houses on right continue ahead along gravel track. Beyond further houses, enter fenced and hedged path with large gravel lake on left. With care cross railway line and go straight on beside hedge, soon reaching the River Thames opposite the lower slopes of Winter Hill (NT).

4 Now turn right along the riverside for 1½ miles, firstly through the water-meadows of Westhorpe Farm and then Wycombe District Council's Riverwoods open space. Finally, follow river through right-hand bend opposite Longridge National Scout Boating Centre and, immediately after passing under large road-bridge, turn right to return to start.

Little Marlow Church

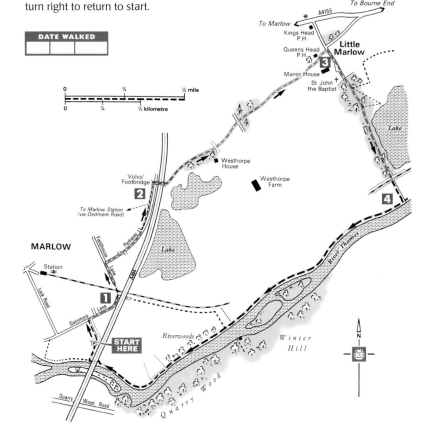

Cookham Dean and Winter Hill

This circular walk takes you through the picturesque area of Cookham Dean, with its attractive 19th-century flint-faced church, and along the top of Winter Hill for some good views of the Chiltern Hills across the Thames Valley.

Distance: 3½ miles

Start: National Trust Cookham Dean Common (free) car park in Winter Hill Road. Grid ref: 862 843

From roadside parking area, follow well-defined path across middle of common towards far right corner where path between trees leads shortly to metalled road. Follow road to junction at Bigfrith Common (NT). Here bear right and after some 30 yards turn right into hedged path between houses – Jay's Oak and Darbys. Soon pass horse barrier and follow rising path through bends to reach gravel track, Pudseys Close, continuing to road ahead. Now turn left (along Spring Lane), becoming

Wayfinding...the family way

Church Road, for over a quarter of a mile, passing the Jolly Farmer on left and the small Victorian church of St John the Baptist on right.

1 At War Memorial, turn left along edge of old Cricket Green (NT), passing Inn on the Green away to left. At bottom of green turn right along gravel track and in far corner turn left down narrow concrete path, Wessons Hill. Shortly, by house on left, Clantock, *keep left* down hedged bridleway to road below (Cookham Dean Bottom).

2 Now turn right along road, soon bearing left at junction, and then at crossroads ahead turn right along Dean Lane using footway on left. At end of houses on left, turn left over concrete step and up gravel farm-track curving right, beside cherry orchard. Approaching buildings, bear left off gravel track and over concrete stile to join drive. After barn turn left, past attractive white cottage, Lea Barn, shortly reaching Winter Hill Road and a glimpse of the views across the Thames Valley.

3 With care turn left along road, but as soon as possible take to verge and grass on right-hand side for the full length of the top of Winter Hill (NT), restored to grass downland with the aid of voluntary working parties. (See map for old ferry crossing point, which can be reached by steep public path here – for the energetic only!) To continue walk, at end of grass area pass through gap in trees ahead and turn right along gravel drive to enter narrow path on right of gate to Rivendell. Follow path beside green wire fence, then take left fork on rising way-marked (white arrows) route through woods to reach fence at boundary. Here turn left for about 15 yards, then right, along narrow fenced path behind gardens, to road junction at top of Quarry Hill Road. Cross road, pass left of large oak tree

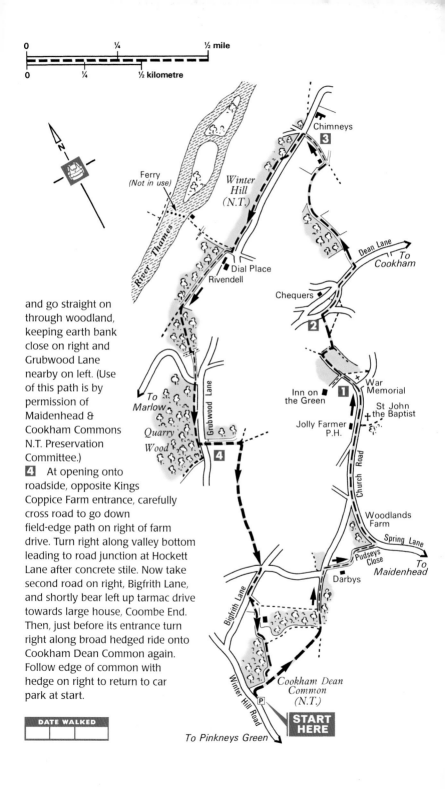

0 — ¼ — ½ mile

0 — ¼ — ½ kilometre

N

Ferry
(Not in use)

Winter
Hill
(N.T.)

Chimneys

3

River Thames

Dean Lane
To
Cookham

Dial Place
Rivendell

Chequers

2

and go straight on through woodland, keeping earth bank close on right and Grubwood Lane nearby on left. (Use of this path is by permission of Maidenhead & Cookham Commons N.T. Preservation Committee.)

War Memorial

Grubwood Lane

Inn on the Green

1

St John the Baptist

Jolly Farmer P.H.

To
Marlow

Quarry
Wood

4

Church Road

Woodlands Farm

Spring Lane

4 At opening onto roadside, opposite Kings Coppice Farm entrance, carefully cross road to go down field-edge path on right of farm drive. Turn right along valley bottom leading to road junction at Hockett Lane after concrete stile. Now take second road on right, Bigfrith Lane, and shortly bear left up tarmac drive towards large house, Coombe End. Then, just before its entrance turn right along broad hedged ride onto Cookham Dean Common again. Follow edge of common with hedge on right to return to car park at start.

Pudseys Close

To
Maidenhead

Darbys

Bigfrith Lane

Winter Hill Road

Cookham Dean
Common
(N.T.)

P

START HERE

To Pinkneys Green

DATE WALKED

Cockmarsh and Quarry Wood

This is the only linear walk in the book: a seven-minute train ride joining the two ends together! (Or you could walk the three miles back along Thames Path.) Enjoy the wonderful views from above Cockmarsh (NT), visit some tucked-away corners of Cookham Dean, and end with a walk through the extensive Quarry Wood, now safely in the hands of the Woodland Trust.

Distance: 5 miles
Start: Bourne End Station.
Grid ref: 894 872

Walk to back of car park beside Platform 2 and enter narrow fenced path. At bottom of steps turn right, pass under bridge and immediately turn left (Thames Path) up steps onto footbridge spanning river. On far bank turn right to a swing-gate, then right again for some 40 yards to cross stile beside gate, turning right under rail

arch to face the N.T. meadows of Cockmarsh. Cockmarsh is part of Maidenhead and Cookham Commons, some 848 acres given to the National Trust in 1934.

1 Head half-left on faint path across the meadows, using the wooden walkway on far side to reach and climb the steep narrow footpath up the hillside ahead. Where this path up the scarp opens out onto grass downland, continue for about 70 yards before bearing left up a further narrow path, leading along top of ridge with golf course over fence on left. Just beyond end of course turn left over stile and cross level field beside hedge on left. At next corner of adjoining golf course enter enclosed path ahead leading to road.

2 Carefully cross road into field-edge path with fence on right and at path junction bear right over stile and continue beside conifer hedge to concrete stile at road. Cross over past

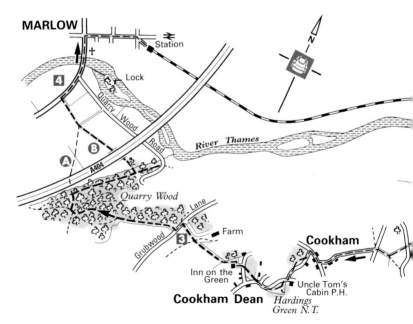

Hillgrove Farm and free-wheel down to bottom of Alleyns Lane. Here continue ahead past garage into Dean Lane for a few yards before turning left up Warners Hill. Within some 60 yards take narrow rising path forking right into copse. Rejoining road, continue to top of slope opposite Uncle Tom's Cabin. Here bear right into Hills Lane and along the edge of (Hardings) Green. Go carefully round double bend in road, passing Popes Lane, and then head across middle of next green on right towards a sign, Inn on the Green. Follow tarmac drive ahead and pass to right of pub, into narrow tree-lined path. Emerging at squeeze-stile go straight ahead on wide grass field-path, down the valley and up the other side to road (Grubwood Lane).

3 Now turn left along road for 50 yards, then right, into Quarry Wood, owned and managed by the Woodland Trust. Follow the wide track ahead, rising slowly, eventually reaching junction of paths. Here go ahead on bridleway, as it forks slightly right, descending steep-sided gully.

Cookham Village

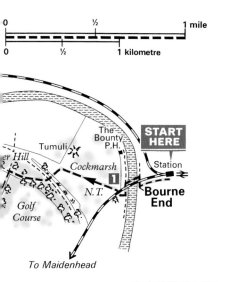

Reaching another 'multiple' junction go ahead, bearing right, into lower of two bridleways, to descend steeply to a crossing track. From this point the historic route **Ⓐ** back across the fields to Marlow is no longer safe (or pleasant!) due to the volume of traffic on the A404. As we go to press, strenuous efforts are being made by the RA to divert the path through a flood tunnel **Ⓑ** under the road. So at this point turn right along the prominent track, with stream below on left. If you find no new path signs on left, continue to end of woods (Parole Bridge) and turn left along right-hand side of Quarry Wood Road, leading to Bisham village.

4 Reaching Bisham, turn right and cross Marlow Bridge. At end of churchyard railings turn right and follow footway to right of green. By mini-roundabout turn right into Station Road. The station is off to the right, a few minutes walk away.

DATE WALKED

Happy Valley and Low Grounds Farm

This circular walk, after leaving the built-up area of Marlow, descends into Happy Valley; then after crossing the Henley Road, continues via Harleyford and Low Grounds Farm, before returning along about 1½ miles of the Thames Path opposite Bisham Abbey.

Distance: 5 miles
Start: Court Garden (pay) car park in Pound Lane, Marlow. Grid ref: 848 862

With your back to car park, at left-hand end, cross road into walled tarmac path (Portland's Alley) to reach West Street, almost opposite Oxford Road. Turn left for about 100 yards to see on left the splendid former Royal Military College and, almost opposite, Shelley's Cottage. Return along West Street and turn left into Oxford Road, then just after Crown and Anchor, turn left into tarmac path. This weaves right and left between sports fields and tennis courts. Reaching road,

cross over and continue straight on, climbing tarmac path. Cross another road to reach a third, Ryans Mount.

1 Here turn sharp left along footway and at end of road pass between metal rails and turn right, to climb wide tarmac path, soon with row of mature trees on left. Cross road ahead and enter path to left of Spinfield School entrance. Follow this enclosed path (soon tarmac) through left and right-hand bends, then turn left into cul-de-sac (Forty Green Drive). At junction ahead turn right into Spinfield Lane, then after last bungalow on left, opposite Bovingdon Heights, turn left along gravel track, soon bearing right to enter path beside metal gate. Follow this narrow path (sadly now fenced) downhill between fields until, just before clump of trees ahead, turn sharp left over stile and descend through middle of field down Happy Valley.

2 Pass ladder-stile on right and in bottom corner of meadow join fenced track down valley, eventually to reach,

Bisham Church in the winter sunshine

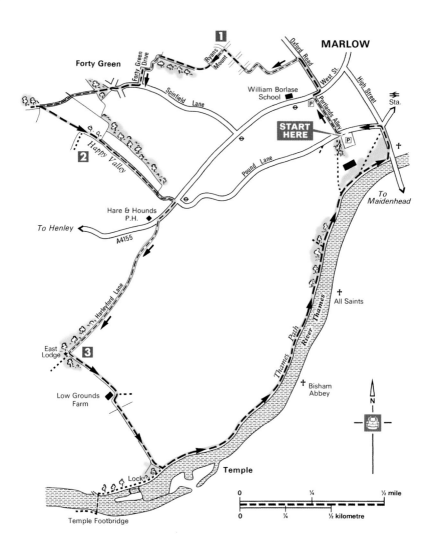

after a nursery and short tarmac drive, the A4155 opposite Pound Lane. With care cross road, turn right along grass verge and opposite Hare & Hounds fork left down private drive (Harleyford Lane), a public footpath.

3 Follow road round sharp left bend (at East Lodge) and pass buildings of Low Grounds Farm. After a right and left-hand bend round the farmhouse wall, track continues ahead to the river. Turn left along the Thames Path for about 1½ miles

to Marlow Bridge, passing on opposite bank the 14th-century Bisham Abbey and Bisham's 12th-century All Saints Church. At Marlow Bridge turn left along paved path with Tierney Court on left, then keep straight on at road ahead, shortly turning left into Pound Lane to return to car park at start.

DATE WALKED		

Thames Path and Temple Footbridge

For many years East Berks RA Group campaigned for a river crossing near Temple (replacing a long-defunct ferry) to avoid a long road detour. A footbridge was finally built in 1989, followed in 1996 by the opening of the Thames Path National Trail.

This ramble follows the Thames Path upstream from Marlow, crosses Temple Bridge to the Berkshire bank, going on to the beautiful and historic village of Hurley, before returning to Marlow.

Distance: 5 miles

Start: Court Garden (pay) car park in Pound Lane, Marlow. Grid ref: 848 862

With your back to car park entrance pass to right of the Court Garden Leisure Complex and follow the tarmac path forking right, with iron railings on left, shortly to reach river. With splendid views of Marlow Church and famous suspension bridge on left, turn right to follow riverside for about 1½ miles to Temple Lock. Look out for several interesting properties on far bank: Stony Ware, an impressive house and grounds, next to Bisham's 12th-century church, and then the 14th-century Bisham Abbey, now the Sports Council's training centre.

1 After passing Temple Lock, cross Temple Bridge and continue now on the Berkshire bank of the river. At end of woodland on left pass through gate into parkland. Follow riverbank to find footbridge in trees and cross to Hurley Lock island. Pass lock, and continue along tarmac path to end of island, to recross main stream by another

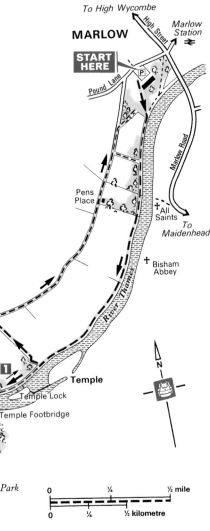

To High Wycombe

Marlow Station

MARLOW

START HERE

Pound Lane

High Street

Marlow Road

Pens Place

All Saints

To Maidenhead

Bisham Abbey

River Thames

Low Grounds Farm

3

Marina

1

Temple

Temple Lock

Temple Footbridge

Hurley Lock

Mill Lane

Shop

2

Hurley

Ye Olde Bell P.H.

Temple Park

N

0 ¼ ½ mile

0 ¼ ½ kilometre

The Temple Footbridge

wooden bridge. Take left-hand steps down from bridge and follow path beside fence and garden wall, soon to reach road. Note on right impressive gatehouse to one-time Tithe Barn, converted into a private residence in 1950 and, beyond the car park wall, the ancient Dovecote built by the monks in 1306.

Temple Lock garden

2 Continue along the road, passing Mill Lane on left. Just before Ye Olde Bell (AD 1135) turn left into narrow footpath, fenced at first, then with fields both sides. At minor road go straight over into narrow hedged path to end of caravan park, then cross stile ahead and continue in same direction now on farm-track. When drive bears right towards white cottage, turn left into fenced path leading shortly to river. Here turn right and retrace your steps over Temple Bridge to lock. Follow broad track from lock, shortly turning sharp left away from river, now with open field on right.

3 Where track bears to right of walled farmhouse, bear right again into grassy farm-track between fenced fields with fine view ahead of high ground (Quarry Wood) in far distance. Cross stile beside metal gate and go straight on, soon joining tree-lined road; pass Pens Place on right and go over a concrete bridge. Ignore first footpath on right but at point where road bears slightly left, bear *right* through gap in wooden fence. Pass through trees and head across sports field to return to car park at start.

DATE WALKED

Hurley Lock and Temple Park

This circular walk is along the Thames Path at Hurley between Frogmill Farm and Temple, and through the adjacent riverside meadows. Within the route are described shorter alternatives of 2½ or 3 miles. At the start, note the attractive largely Norman church of St Mary the Virgin and, behind the car park wall (fast disappearing behind conifers), the Dovecote built by the monks in 1306 and the old Tithe Barn converted into a private residence in 1950.

Distance: 2½, 3 or 4 miles

Start: Free car park in Hurley village, opposite the Church. Grid ref: 825 840

With your back to the church, leave car park in far left-hand corner to enter short walled path. After stile keep straight on along lane with caravan site on right and fields on left. After boat-park, go 60 yards beyond large oak overhanging road and turn left over stile, following field edge with hedge on right. Leave field by stile to right of house ahead and shortly turn right along the narrow Shepherds Lane.

1 Where lane turns left, keep straight on along track towards Shepherds Cottage*. Follow path skirting to right of cottage, with hedge on left, and maintain same direction through middle of field towards stile in hedge on Henley Road. Do *not* climb this stile, but turn half-right to stile in hedge on far side of field. After stile continue in same direction through middle of next field to reach stile at rear of second white house from left, Sungei Lalu, on far side of field. The public path passes through this property, so follow concrete path with brick wall on right, go through gate beside house and along edge of front lawn to the riverside and turn right along the towpath.

At end of houses, pass through stileway next to gate, shortly to observe Danesfield, the large white house on the hill among trees, overlooking the stretch of river ahead. Built in 1899/1901

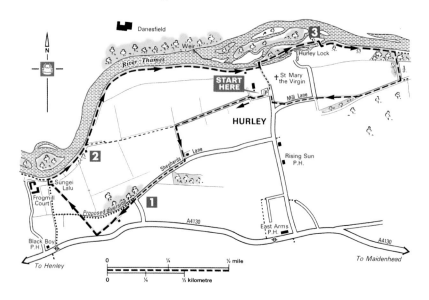

Footbridge from the lock island at Hurley

for Robert Hudson, wealthy son of a
Victorian soap magnate, it is now a
hotel.

2 After old white-painted cottage
known as Poisson Duc (the Norman-
French for pike), pass beside gate
and bear left to follow riverside
through meadows for nearly a mile.
Opposite weir pass through swing-gate
on riverbank and keeping along
water's edge, finally leave meadow
by small iron gate. Cross narrow
footbridge and continue to foot of
large wooden bridge. If you wish
only to do the 2½-mile walk, turn right
down steps at this point, and along
tarmac path back to the start.

    To continue the longer walks,
cross river by the large wooden bridge
and turn right past Hurley Lock. For the
3-mile walk, turn right over second
lock gate to enter narrow path leading
to Mill Lane. Follow road and keep
turning right to return to start.

3 To continue longest walk, from

the lock-island cross the second
wooden bridge to return to south
side of river and turn left along
riverbank. At end of second field,
path continues with woodland on
right. After about 130 yards, with
Temple Bridge in sight, turn right
through this wood along narrow
fenced path leading to Temple Park.
Here turn right along surfaced drive.
75 yards after passing through
gateway with cattle-grid, bear right
over stile and immediately right again,
on broad grass strip, straight through
caravan park. Cross drive ahead and
leave park through gap to left of
gateway. Maintain same direction
in lane ahead, shortly turning right
to return to car park at start.

** There is a diversion proposal for this
path at time of publication (see map).*

DATE WALKED		

Hodgedale Lane and Prospect Hill

This circular walk begins along a fine stretch of the Thames Path and then climbs gently to the hills overlooking the river valley, passing across land farmed by the Berkshire College of Agriculture.

Distance: 5 miles
Start: Hurley village free car park, opposite Church. Grid ref: 825 840

At start, you may just see between fast-growing conifers over car park wall the former Tithe Barn, converted to a private residence in 1950, and a Dovecote built by the monks in 1306.

Facing the attractive, largely Norman Church of St Mary the Virgin, leave car park, turning left along tarmac path. A few yards before footbridge over river, turn left on gravel path and join riverbank. Shortly cross wooden footbridge and pass through metal swing-gate to follow riverbank ahead for nearly one mile.

Along this stretch, on hilltop on far side of river, look out for large white building – Danesfield, built 1899/1901 for Robert Hudson, wealthy son of a Victorian soap magnate. It is now a hotel.

1 At end of this long meadow a swing-gate leads into narrow field and a gap in front of bungalow soon brings you to an old white-painted cottage (called Poison Duc, Norman-French for pike). Continue, now on gravel path, with moorings on right. At end of chalets on left, pass through stileway by metal gate. Opposite the last semi-detached house shortly on left, bear right to follow grassy path on river's edge in front of converted farm buildings (now Frogmill Court). At end of lawned area, turn sharp left away from river to reach road.

Follow this lane to reach the Black Boy. Turn left in front of pub and with great care cross road (A4130), now to follow a steadily rising path (Hodgedale Lane) between fields, with fine views particularly on left.

2 At top of slope continue on level ground to a path junction. Here follow stone way-mark pointing left, inscribed: 'Public Bridleway to Honey Lane'. Between the two paths (access from the right) is a Nature Reserve, cared for by BBONT (Bucks, Berks & Oxon Naturalists' Trust). Follow meandering path through trees with field close-by on left. Emerging from woodland at wooden gate continue on grassy track between fields. The tidy paddocks away to right belong to the Arab-owned Juddemonte Stud, home to the cream of equine bloodstock. After metal gate join a concrete track for about 150 yards and at path junction turn left into fenced grassy track. (Before buildings of Top Farm ahead there is a path on right to the Dewdrop Inn.)

3 Our route along this right of way used to run straight ahead but was diverted in 1996 to avoid the farmyard.

The Ramblers' Association protects your right to walk in the countryside

The Ramblers

You can help by becoming a member
Write to:
1/5 Wandsworth Road, London, SW8 2XX
Telephone: 0171 339 8500

So just before the barn, turn left and then shortly right, on line of new bridleway. Cross lane, stepping a few yards left to continue in same direction. Notice small plaque here describing a pole gate. This farm road is a 'Permitted Path' which is the effective answer for the landowner who is happy to see genuine ramblers enjoying the countryside, but who nevertheless does not want a right of way established across the land.

4 Look out for crossing path and here turn left on grassy track leading straight across the fields to stile into High Wood.

Path continues to further stile at top of Prospect Hill. From here go straight down towards Hurley village in the valley. While admiring the view, do walk with care, as the path is rather steep and can be slippery at times.

At bottom of path, carefully cross road at East Arms (A4130) and then follow High Street ahead, passing Rising Sun and Ye Olde Bell (AD 1135) to return to car park at start.

DATE WALKED

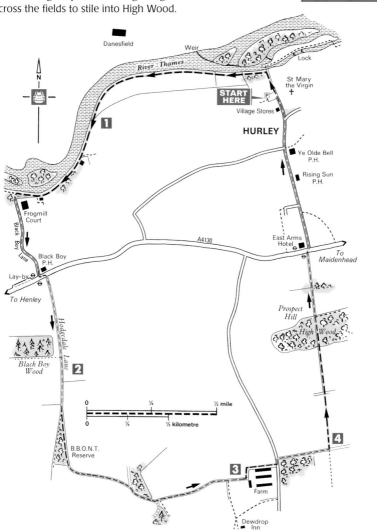

Rose Lane and Culham Farms

This circular walk crosses the rich undulating farmland between Henley and Hurley and follows the Thames Path National Trail for a mile.

Distance: 5 miles

Start: North side of Cockpole Green. Grid ref: 800 812 Parking is easier on lanes to south of Green.

From north side of Cockpole Green, enter concrete track signposted 'Public Bridleway' to pass by the buildings of Goulders Farm and then along farm-track. The distant large white building on far side of Thames Valley is Danesfield. Built 1899/1901 for Robert Hudson, wealthy son of a Victorian soap magnate, it is now a hotel. Continue down hedged track with woodland (Goulders Shaw) soon on left. (The building in fold of land to your right is Dean Place, at the other end of 'Permitted Path' on right.) At end of wood follow right turn in path for about 30 yards, then turn left along Rose Lane, passing 'Rosehill', leading to main road.

The paddocks on right of lane form the superb Juddemonte Stud, an equine paradise for the cream of English racing bloodstock bred here.

1 With extreme care cross the main road (A4130) ahead, then turn left along gravel track through Lodge gateway, and just after storage yard on right, turn right down bank to follow edge of field with hedge and fence on left. Cross over farm-track near end of this large field and shortly enter meadow ahead, to reach the River Thames. Now turn left through swing-gate to follow Thames Path signs through three fields and then along a track.

2 Just beyond cottages on right, bear left where the way divides and, leaving Thames Path, continue ahead along track, passing Culham Court away to right. This large red-brick house, restored in the 1930s, was built in 1771 and in the grounds is one of the best alpine rock gardens in the country. At junction with drive up to house, turn left up tarmac road and shortly after fenced copse on left, turn right onto broad grass cross-field path. On far side keep to wide field-edge path bearing left, with woodland on right. At top of climb turn right through gap in hedge and then immediately left, along edge of field with hedge on left.

Local **RA** Group members on the headland path near Culham

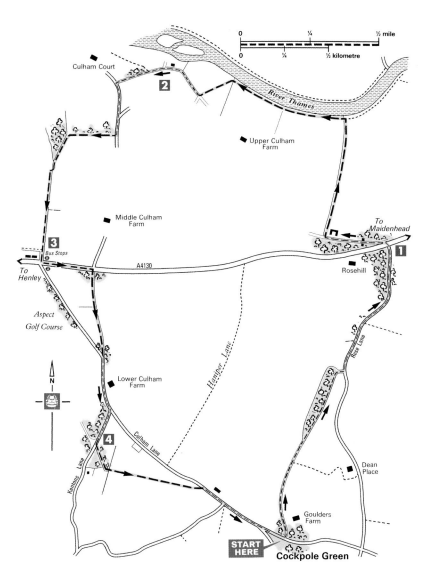

0 ¼ ½ mile
0 ¼ ½ kilometre

Culham Court

2

River Thames

Upper Culham Farm

Middle Culham Farm

3 Bus Stops

To Henley

A4130

Rosehill

1

To Maidenhead

Aspect Golf Course

Hennifer Lane

Rose Lane

N

Lower Culham Farm

Kentons Lane

Culham Lane

4

Dean Place

Goulders Farm

START HERE
Cockpole Green

3 On reaching houses keep straight on along short 'Permitted Path' to road (A4130) ahead. Here turn left for about 300 yards, then with care turn right across road and over stile along wide grass track with fence and then hedge on left. At end of field, continue ahead on short track to road and then keep to grass verge on right to reach road junction, here turn right along Kentons Lane towards Wargrave.

4 At end of field on left, opposite Pillar Lodge, turn left through swing-gate. At end of hedge on right bear left to swing-gate and continue through middle of large field towards distant houses. At road (Culham Lane) turn right to return to Cockpole Green and the start.

DATE WALKED		

Aston and Remenham

This circular walk climbs to follow the high ground overlooking the Greenlands Estate before returning along the Thames Path from Remenham to Aston. The Estate is the largest single area protected by National Trust covenants, given by the third Viscount Hambleden in 1944 to protect the landscape and buildings between and around the villages of Hambleden and Remenham.

Distance: 4¼ miles
Start: Car park (small charge) at Mill End, Hambleden, near Henley-on-Thames. Grid ref: 785 854

Leave car park and turn right along footway. At junction with A4155 keep right of verge before carefully crossing main road, into footpath to right of cottage.

Go ahead onto the 300m walkway over the weir, in front of the much painted and photographed white weather-boarded Hambleden Mill. It dates from 1338 and is now converted into apartments. Reaching the lock, enlarged and rebuilt in 1996 at a cost of £1.9 million, turn left along the riverside.

Morning mist Photo by Clive Ormonde

1 Where gravel drive to lock turns away from river, go through metal gate ahead into riverside meadow, at the far end of which a wooden swing-gate leads to roadway. Here note remaining evidence on both riverbanks of the long-ceased Aston Ferry.

2 Turn right along lane (Aston Ferry Lane) and on reaching Flower Pot Hotel at Aston, bear slightly left to continue up narrow hedged road (Aston Lane). Immediately after Highway Cottage on right, turn right up bank to climb enclosed path with stone wall on right at first. After stile, carry on up hill to leave paddock through gap in hedge and continue ahead along farm-track. Follow this track for about ½ mile between large fields − part of Greenlands Estate − then on reaching road ahead (Church Lane), turn right along road and down hill to the small Victorian Gothic church of Remenham.

3 Here turn right and follow narrow lane beside church wall, then shortly bear left along gravel track, with converted barns on left, to reach River Thames after swing-gate. Now turn right along river bank for nearly two miles (surfaced most of the way), passing firstly Temple Island, then Greenlands on the opposite bank.

Shortly in mid-stream is the one-acre Temple Island with a Georgian folly designed by James Wyatt at its southern end − the start of the straight Henley Royal Regatta course that runs for 1 mile 550 yards to just below Henley Bridge. The regatta was established in 1839 after the first Oxford and Cambridge boat race was rowed between Hambleden Lock and Henley Bridge in 1829 − the event became 'Royal' in 1851. Further on, the white Victorian Italianate mansion on the far bank, with well-groomed lawns down to the river's edge, is Greenlands − now Henley Management College − built mainly in 1871 by the W H Smith family.

Reaching the Hambleden lock, turn left over the lock gates and retrace your steps back to the car park at Mill End.

DATE WALKED		

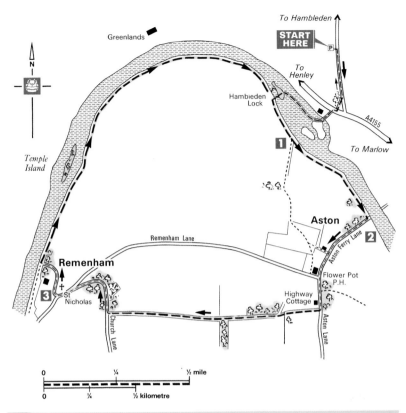

Henley at dawn *Photo by Clive Ormonde*

If you have enjoyed these walks and feel encouraged to follow the whole length of the River Thames from its source in the Cotswolds to the Thames Barrier in London (180 miles/288 km), see the **National Trail Guide: The Thames Path** *by David Sharp.*

Culham Court and Henley Reach

This circular walk provides fine views of the Chiltern Hills across the Thames Valley. It goes out through the woodland at Remenham Hill, passes through the fields of Culham Farms and returns along that reach of the River Thames used for Henley Royal Regatta.

Distance: 6 miles
Start: From the bridge at Henley-on-Thames. Grid ref: 764 826

From Henley Bridge, walk along left-hand footway of A4130 towards Maidenhead, passing the Little Angel, the cricket ground and then allotments below on left. At end of footway turn left up steps into woodland. Shortly cross drive and continue climbing path between iron railings. Entering Remenham Woods ahead, follow the well-defined path which soon crosses a gravel track and eventually follows a long wooden fence on left to property, Whitewood House, at road. Turn left along road (Church Lane) for about 20 yards, then turn right through small wooden gate and across middle of two fields, with fine views beyond Woodside Farm to the left. At far side of field, turn right through small wooden gate into well-defined winding woodland path. On reaching white gateposts to private drive, go past them turning sharp left along gravel drive (to Yewgate Cottage). At concrete posts go straight on, with fence and meadows on left, to arrive with care at road ahead.

1 Turn right along road (Aston Lane) to junction with main road (A4130). Here turn left over stile into corner of field and follow field-edge through left and right-hand bends with conifers and houses on right. At end of houses, turn left into track along side of field with large trees and, later, hedge on right. Just before copse ahead, turn right through gap in hedge and continue in same direction, now with hedge, then copse, on left. At corner of copse, path bears right on tree-dotted grass track between fields. Reaching stile onto estate road turn left and shortly fork left at small clump of fenced trees. At bottom of dip in drive to Culham Court, turn sharp right and then shortly before the end of the meadow on left, turn left through gate to join the Thames Path (now a National Trail).

2 After two small fields the path leads via a series of swing-gates through the grounds of Culham Court, an impressive red-brick mansion built in 1771 and restored in the 1930s. Now continue straight ahead through middle of long narrow field to iron gate just left of distant house (Holme Farm), then follow drive down to road (Aston Lane), near the popular Flower Pot Hotel.

3 Turn left up the lane and immediately after Highway Cottage on right, turn right up bank to climb enclosed path with stone wall and then hedge on right. After stile, continue up hill to leave field through gap in hedge. Continue ahead along gravel track. The land ahead is part of the Greenlands Estate covenants – over 3,900 acres were given to the National Trust by the third Viscount Hambleden in 1944 to protect the landscape and buildings between and around the villages of Hambleden and Remenham. Continue along this track for about ½ mile between large fields and on reaching road (Church Lane), turn right along road and down hill to Remenham Church. Follow church wall round to right and continue along road, then gravel track, leading to the River Thames and the world-famous Royal Regatta course along Henley Reach.

4 Now turn left and follow the river all the way back to the bridge at Henley.

DATE WALKED		

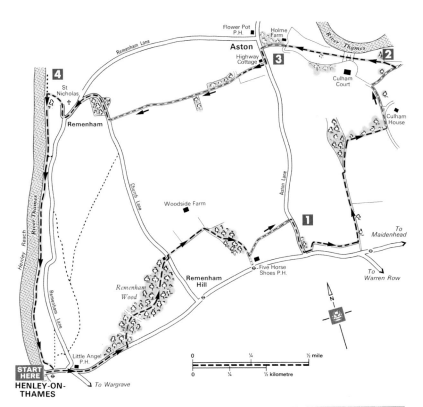

The Regatta Course, looking towards Temple Island

Remenham Wood and Mill End

This circular walk provides high - level views from Remenham Hill of the distant Chilterns, visits the picturesque Hambleden Mill at Mill End and returns along the west bank of that reach of the River Thames famed for Henley Royal Regatta. In winter and after heavy rain, the water-meadows can be rather wet underfoot.

Distance: 6½ miles

Start: Car park (free on Sundays) in Kings Road, Henley. Grid ref: 759 828

With your back to Waitrose, leave car park at far left-hand exit, turn left along Kings Road and left again down Market Place and Hart Street to Henley Bridge, just beyond the Parish Church of St Mary the Virgin. Note plaque on end of bridge to engine drivers! About 35 yards beyond far end of bridge, turn left down tarmac road and follow car park railings round to right, to reach road through gap in hedge. Cross road, pass through swing-gate and head for stile in hedge, to left of low bank. Follow slightly raised path through middle of small golf course. On far side notice at ground level memorial to 'Minty'.

1 Cross stile just ahead in trees and, keeping slightly left, continue through small copse. On emerging into bottom of field near corner of fence on left, bear right up slope of meadow and over stile into Remenham Wood and along well-defined grassy path. At end of woodland, go half-right up slope through middle of large field and as path rises, aim for road (Church Lane) just to left of solitary oak tree ahead. Turn left along road, then just before woodland ahead, turn right at stile next to gate and join gravel farm-track between large fields, part of

the Greenlands Estate covenants − over 3,900 acres were given to the National Trust in 1944 by the third Viscount Hambleden.

2 Eventually, where track turns left, keep straight on through gap in hedge and down left side of two small fields to road, by Highway Cottage. Turn left down lane, pass to right of Flower Pot Hotel into Aston Ferry Lane and immediately before cottage on left, turn left into hedged path. Cross field corner ahead before turning right along gravel drive leading to River Thames and Hambleden Lock. The lock was enlarged and rebuilt in 1996 at a cost of £1.9 million.

3 Here turn right over the lower lock gate and follow the 300-yard footway over the weir to Hambleden Mill, dating from 1338, now converted into apartments. Keeping fence and then hedge of Mill House on left, continue ahead to road. Here with great care cross over, turning right, then shortly left, towards Hambleden village. At turning on right, *turn left* up gravel track, cross stile ahead and go straight on through middle of two fields towards distant red-roofed cottage, to reach stile at main road (A4155). Here with great care turn right along road keeping to right-hand verge where possible. Just after entrance to Greenlands (Henley Management College) cross road and continue along footway on left.

4 Find stile on left in parkland fence and follow chain of wooden footbridges linking these Thames-side water-meadows for some 1½ miles. Notice in mid-stream, Temple Island, with ornamental fishing lodge built in 1771 by James Wyatt, marking the start of the Henley Royal Regatta course. The red-brick mansion at end of avenue of poplars on the right is Fawley Court, built in 1684 by Sir Christopher Wren.

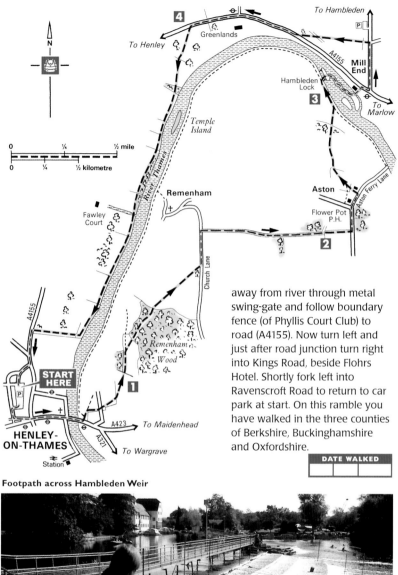

away from river through metal swing-gate and follow boundary fence (of Phyllis Court Club) to road (A4155). Now turn left and just after road junction turn right into Kings Road, beside Flohrs Hotel. Shortly fork left into Ravenscroft Road to return to car park at start. On this ramble you have walked in the three counties of Berkshire, Buckinghamshire and Oxfordshire.

DATE WALKED

Footpath across Hambleden Weir

Harpsden Wood and Marsh Lock

This circular walk, to the south of Henley-on-Thames, climbs up through Harpsden and its beautiful background of beech woodland, descends across the fields to Lower Shiplake, and returns along the Thames Path National Trail and over the long wooden bridges at Marsh Lock.

This walk was first published by the Ramblers' Association in 1980 – the year chosen to promote 'Footpath Heritage 80', a campaign to encourage people to use and enjoy our heritage of public paths. Since then, membership of the RA has more than trebled.

Distance: 4 miles
Start: Free car park in Mill Lane, Henley-on-Thames.
Grid ref: 771 817

The path through Harpsden Wood

Leaving car park, turn right along Mill Lane, pass over railway bridge and with care cross main road (A4155) into Waterman's Road. Shortly, at concrete posts ahead, enter tree-lined bridleway with houses on right. At road ahead turn left along Harpsden Way, on right-hand footway, to reach in about ¼ mile on left the Tudor Harpsden Court and the attractive 12th-century flint-faced parish church of St Margaret's. Opposite church, notice on end walls of barn to Harpsden Court Farm, old wooden printing blocks once used in wallpaper manufacture.

1 Just before gate to cemetery ahead, turn left into narrow path on left of, and at first parallel to, Woodlands Road. At top of steep gully fork left to follow remains of fence on left. On reaching road again, keep straight on (where possible on woodland verge) and where road bends left, cross over by entrance to Red Hatch Lodge to enter narrow path through woods, now with laurel hedge on left. Reaching road, turn left and at junction shortly ahead, cross over and pass to left of Little Beeches. Follow winding gravel bridleway descending to reach the road (A4155) by Engbers garden-centre (coffee shop here!)

2 With care cross road and take fenced field-path, then continue along road (Northfield Avenue). Reaching road junction at the Baskerville Arms, turn *sharp left* into cul-de-sac and shortly enter narrow hedged path to right of garage. Carefully cross railway line stiles and bear left through metal swing-gate into fenced path. Keep *straight on* across gravel drive and lawn, then turn left (Bolney Road). At far end of road keep left of gateway, into narrow path beside drive, following Thames Path sign. Continue ahead, soon with wire

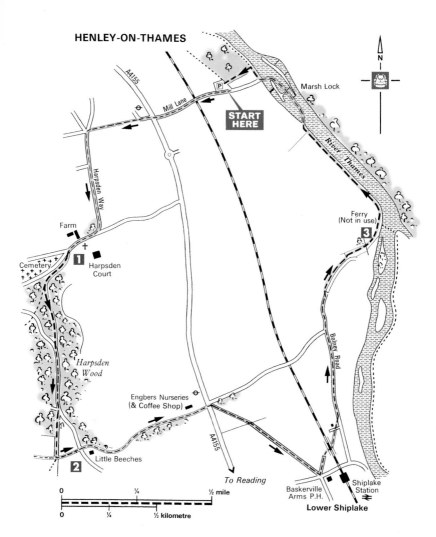

HENLEY-ON-THAMES

Marsh Lock

START HERE

River Thames

Ferry (Not in use)

3

Harpsden Way

Farm

Cemetery

1

Harpsden Court

Harpsden Wood

Bolney Road

Engbers Nurseries (& Coffee Shop)

A4155

Little Beeches

2

To Reading

Baskerville Arms P.H.

Shiplake Station

Lower Shiplake

```
0          ¼          ½ mile
0          ¼          ½ kilometre
```

fences both sides of path to cross stile and plank footbridge over ditch.
3 Cross meadow to River Thames just ahead (site of one-time Bolney Ferry), and bear left along river bank – Cottage Reach. On the far bank notice Conways Bridge, named after General Conway and reputed to be built of stones taken from Reading Abbey. The Victorian boat-house here once belonged to Park Place mansion on the hill above.

At end of meadow, bear right over long wooden footbridge to Marsh Lock

and return to the same bank via a second bridge. The original bridges and lock were built about 1770 by Humphrey Gainsborough, brother of the famous artist, Thomas. Reaching the riverside at the end of Mill Lane, turn right for about 80 yards before turning left along edge of meadow to return to car park at start.

DATE WALKED

Wargrave and Hennerton Backwater

This walk meanders around the older part of Wargrave village, then after crossing Hennerton Backwater, heads north on the old Thames towpath, now a cul-de-sac, along the edge of Wargrave Marsh.

Distance: 5 miles

Start: Car park in School Lane, Wargrave. Grid ref: 786 786

With your back to car park, turn left up School Lane for just over 150 yards, then turn right into Spring Walk and follow road curving left. Shortly at junction with Braybrooke Road turn right. Immediately after No. 44 The Chestnuts, turn left to visit cemetery in old chalk pit, or to continue walk, turn right down broad tree-lined track.

1 At main road (A321) ahead, turn right for about 75 yards, then with care cross over into Station Road. Just after the end of brick and flint wall on right, turn right on tarmac path along edge of Green. To the left is the attractive flint and brick Parish Church of St Mary's, rebuilt in 1916 after being

Parish Council landing stage

almost completely destroyed by fire on the night of June 1, 1914. The War Memorial on the Green was designed by Sir Edwin Lutyens.

2 In the far corner of the Green, pass through metal swing-gate and continue along road (Church Street) for about 25 yards. Here keep straight on to continue the walk, or turn left into Ferry Lane, and shortly left again (opposite Ferry Cottage) down gravel track, for access to, and a different view of, the River Thames at the Parish Council's landing stage for light craft.

Continuing in Church Street turn left at traffic lights along High Street,

Backsideans

then look for two other access points to the river. The first, about 40 yards beyond turning by Wargrave Motors, is the walled path on left, between 6A High Street and Ferry House. The second is behind the St George & Dragon, site of the one-time ferry. From here, access to the riverside paths in the meadows opposite is usually only possible once a year, during the Wargrave & Shiplake Regatta.

3 Continue along main road ahead, using footway on right. Set in deer park, the large white house (Wargrave Manor) is a residence of the Sultan of Oman. On reaching roadside properties, with care turn left across road into Willow Lane (a public footpath). Shortly cross Hennerton Backwater (the longest backwater on the Thames) and continue to end of lane. Immediately after the property Mallards, turn left into fenced gravel path leading to the River Thames. Here turn right along the old towpath with riverside properties of Shiplake on the far bank. Eventually enter field after gate and continue to follow riverbank along edge of Wargrave Marsh. At field boundary pass through another gate and, water level permitting, keep along edge of woodland to soon reach other end of Hennerton Backwater, and the site of the one-time Bolney Ferry.

4 Now retrace your steps along the river, Willow Lane and main road, then shortly after the St George & Dragon, turn left up Wargrave Hill. About 75 yards up the hill turn right into tarmac drive. At entrance to Woodclyffe Almshouses keep right along narrow path with high brick wall on right. Follow path through left-hand bend and in ten yards turn right down road (Backsideans), shortly to reach on right car park at start.

Bolney Ferry
(Not in use)

To Henley

A321

N

Hennerton Backwater

Wargrave Marsh

Lashbrook Ferry
(Not in use)

River Thames

Willow Lane

0   ¼ mile
0   ¼ kilometre

Wargrave Manor

3

Ferry
(See Text)

St George & Dragon

Shiplake

Ferry Lane

P   School Lane

2 START HERE

St Marys

Station Road

Wargrave Station

A321

1

Cemetery

WARGRAVE

To Twyford

DATE WALKED

Binfield Heath and Shiplake College

This circular walk between Sonning and Shiplake goes out through the farmland around Binfield Heath that overlooks the Thames Valley, and returns along two miles of the Thames Path National Trail on the Oxfordshire bank.

Distance: 6 miles
Start: From small parking area opposite French Horn.
Grid ref: 753 759
Parking also possible in cul-de-sac nearby – see map.

With your back to the French Horn take the narrow walled path (old name – Furleigh Path) behind the car park, then turn left and shortly right on quiet lane through Sonning Eye (meaning 'island'). At junction keep straight on to end of cul-de-sac and cross busy road (B478) into road opposite (Poolspring Lane). Beware of one-way traffic! At start of second field on right cross stile and follow field edge. Before end of next field, rejoin the lane to Flowing Spring.

1 Carefully cross main road (A4155), climb steps ahead and turn right along field edge (a new 'Permitted Path' instigated in 1996 by the authors to avoid the hazardous road). Just short

of field end join old road and turn sharp left on bridleway up south-eastern face of the Chiltern Hills as they billow up from the valley. Keep climbing, ignoring left fork, finally to reach road at Binfield Heath opposite Dragon Cottage (formerly George & Dragon pub).

2 Here turn right and some 90 paces beyond postbox turn right down side of two fields, with kissing gate in-between, and into Shiplake Copse on descending woodland path – a carpet of bluebells in early May. Emerging from trees bear left along field edge.

3 Shortly, where field boundary swings left, maintain direction across corner of field to rejoin headland. Cross sunken track and bear slightly right through middle of next field to electricity pole, with fine views ahead, including Bowsey Hill.

By the pole turn left between fields. At clump of trees a path bears left (to White Hart) but our way goes straight on for about 100 yards, then turns right along edge of field with fence on left. On reaching stile with concrete step turn left, now with fence on right. Leave this field via iron kissing gate, bear left on farm drive and turn right along road (Plough Lane).

4 At Plowden Arms with care cross road (A4155) into Church Lane leading past attractive flint-faced Shiplake Parish Church of St Peter & St Paul where Tennyson was married on June 13, 1850. Nearby are the red-brick buildings of Shiplake College.

After the church, bear right down gravel track with occasional steps, then where farm-track appears on right, turn left, shortly to reach river. Now turn right over footbridge to follow Thames Path for about two miles to reach Sonning Bridge and to return to the start.

Rowing practice for a young College crew

DATE WALKED		